Memories of a Village Historian

By Peter West, Brome and Oakley

Copyright

All rights reserved. No part of this publication may be reproduced, stored in a retrieval system, or transmitted in any form or by any means, electronic, mechanical, photocopying, recording or otherwise without prior permission of the author or his agents.

ISBN 978-1-3999-8004-3

Foreword

The history of a place and its people is important. It shapes our lives and our landscape. This book is my effort to record some of the history of Brome & Oakley and its neighbouring parishes. As anyone who knows me will be aware I have a huge stock of historical facts and interpretations in my memory. This is my effort at committing them to print. In this I have been greatly helped by Jennie Barfield, a family member who was born and brought up in Brome and who undertook the daunting task of taking my rough notes through to first drafts. Subsequently John Parry helped with researching and editing text and pictures. I am extremely grateful to both for their help.

About the author

Peter West has farmed in Brome and nearby all his life. His grandfather Charles Augustus West was originally from Sussex and moved to Warren Hills in Brome in 1908, originally as tenants of Brome and Oakley estate. His mother was Hannah Arete Flowerdew, part of that East Anglian dynasty which arrived shortly after William the Conqueror and have farmed here ever since. Peter farmed the land from the 1940s and only recently stepped back. His professional life included representing UK farming in Whitehall and Brussels when the UK was part of the EEC and EU. He held various positions with the National Farmers Union in Suffolk and Norfolk including a spell as chairman of Norfolk NFU. More locally he has been an active and valued supporter of village organisations such as the Parish Council, the Village Hall and Community Club, and the Parochial Church Council. He was an active member of Eye Tennis Club and a major supporter when it transformed into Eye Bowls Club, where he served as president. His interest in local history runs deep; he sees the history in the landscape, the buildings and the people who made them. His previous publication (2010) was *Memories of a Farmer, 100 years of C A West & Son*.

Introduction

My family has farmed in and around Brome & Oakley for more than a hundred years. The area is steeped in history. The A140 bordering its western side was originally an important Roman road which crossed the Waveney near its head of navigation. Later Saxon occupations would have arrived by sea initially then settled to live off the rich farming land. After the Normans arrived in 1066 their barons and churches built off the wealth of the area until the plagues of the 14th century emptied the villages.

Slowly the populations rebuilt with farming again dominating the area through the development of the big estates and grand houses. Hoxne Hall was one, Brome Hall was another, with its owners writing themselves into the pages of world history and attracting attention from the kings and queens of England.

The wars and social upheavals of the 20th century brought that era of wealth, power and privilege to an end and again Brome and Oakley were directly involved; initially hosting WW1 cavalry regiments then in WW2 a British Army base and the US Air Force base, parts of which survive today.

All this history leaves its marks. I have seen the archaeology in the river banks, the old churches, the settlements and the fields. I was directly involved in sorting through centuries of records of the Kerrison estate and the old Benedictine Abbey in Eye, now Abbey Farm. And a lifetime ago I rode in US Air Force Flying Fortresses and listened to the pre-dawn chorus of their engines warming up for missions to Germany, some never to return.

This book is my effort at chronicling this history. It is not an A-Z story, rather it is a series of pictures and memories of what has happened in Brome and Oakley and nearby from someone who's daily life was working in a landscape shaped by two thousand years of nobles, churchmen, soldiers, landowners and the men and women who tilled, sowed and harvested the land.

CONTENTS

CHAPTER ONE – the first 1,000 years 1

The Romans settle – Basil Brown 1

Three settlements - Professor David Trump 1

Early Saxon presence 2

CHAPTER TWO – The Normans make their mark 1066 to 1400 3

The Normans take over 3

Barons and churchmen make their mark – Eye Abbey 3

CHAPTER THREE – the era of Estates 1400 – 1900 9

Brome Hall and the Cornwallis family 9

Boke of Brome 10

An English martyr 11

Estate life under the Kerrisons 13

CHAPTER FOUR – a time of change 28

Village life 28

A local hero – Lt Gordon Flowerdew 29

Mechanisation on the farms 30

Schooldays in Brome 30

CHAPTER FIVE – 1939 onwards 51

The friendly invasion 51

Eye airfield 51

The 490 Bomb Group 52

Chapter 1 – The first 1000 years

During the Roman period, Scole was the largest settlement in the area. It was a staging post on the main Roman road between the garrison towns of Colchester and Caistor St Edmund (near Norwich). The Romans were clearly settled and active in the area with remains, currency hordes and artefacts being found in Oakley, Hoxne and Eye.

Basil Brown, the Suffolk archaeologist, came to Warren Hill farm in Oakley and Stuston in 1938 with the intention of digging and surveying the Suffolk side of the river Waveney near Scole. Although there is no modern settlement there he believed that the Romans settled both sides of the River Waveney. His findings proved that was correct. There were a further two surveys carried out before the road changes took place on the Suffolk side. These surveys revealed evidence of both an Iron Age and Roman settlement, with a brewery, wells and proof of barley being cultivated near the river.

One interesting question is whether the Waveney was navigable to Scole two thousand years ago, adding to Scole's importance. The Roman road which came from Colchester to Caistor St Edmund had a branch which went eastwards from Scole for 400 yards. This branch finished in the field we know as the Dock Meadow, part of Warren Hill farm next to the Waveney. Unknown to the archaeologists, I had witnessed river dredging in the 1950s which revealed decaying timbers along the side of dock meadow, most probably Roman river quayside facilities.

Basil Brown was born near Ipswich and brought up in Rickinghall. His archaeology was initially self taught and later supported by Ipswich Museum. After his excavation work in this area Basil Brown moved on. He became famous for his Sutton Hoo discovery in 1939 where he excavated a burial ship of the famous Saxon King Radwaeld along with all his treasures. The museum on the site is well worth the visit.

Three settlements

The Saxon period, from around 400 A.D. to the Norman conquest in 1066, has also left its mark on the area, though you have to look harder for the signs. Brome and Oakley, now one village under local authority definitions, were previously three settlements. The original centre of Brome was probably around Brome church. There are ancient building foundations around about and sections of Saxon masonry in what is mainly a Norman round tower embedded in Brome Church.

But there were two Oakley villages; Oakley Parva ('Parva' is Latin for small) and Oakley Magna (meaning either larger or upper). In the 1970s Dr David H Trump and Dr Bridget Trump, two retired Cambridge University academics, came to the area as part of their research into the lost parishes of East Anglia. Specifically they were searching for the site of the lost parish of Oakley Parva. After extensive searches they discovered remains in the vicinity of the Alder Carr near the River Waveney. The site was Saxon in origin and was still in existence until 1430 when the village was amalgamated with Oakley Magna, whereupon Oakley became one village with one church and one parson. The Trumps also found evidence of a small, very early Saxon church to the north of Poplar Farm in Lower Oakley. Dr David Trump was a leading figure in British archeology. His professional expertise was the archeology of Malta but in his retirement took up researching East Anglian sites. He was also an early pioneer of carbon dating.

Until 1948 there was a very large gravel pit to the north of the present Oakley Church. During 1943-46 this pit was filled with refuse from the Brome and Thorpe Abbotts airfields. Bulldozing topsoil over the site later revealed the 'lost' village of Oakley Magna, which would have been centred around the existing church. Archaeologists were soon called to the quite substantial site. There were indications that it also contained a 'plague pit', which might indicate the village was abandoned in the fifteenth century, along with Oakley Parva, as a result of the Black Death.

Probably the main visual evidence of the Saxon presence is to be found in the meadows near where the River Waveney and Dove flow towards Hoxne. Here are 'Doles', strips of raised fields from several centuries of strip farming. Begun in Saxon times the system persisted until well after the Norman takeover and provided some degree of self-sufficiency for the villagers in the area. An 1838 survey map of the area also indicates a 'pest house' i.e. an isolation house for those unfortunate to fall ill from disease.

In Brome archaeologists spent one summer digging and researching the moat near Brome church. They found that it had existed for a considerable amount of time and was originally Saxon. There was evidence of several buildings that were still occupied in the 12th century with indications that this was where the main population of the village of Brome was centred. A number of artefacts were recovered from the excavation.

There are also references in the Doomsday book to a Dame Gode, a Saxon, in the area. She owned the equivalent to 200 acres in the area, possibly around Warren Hill farm. After 1066 this land was granted to the Norman lord Roger Bigod, who then went on to build both Bungay and Framlingham castles.

Chapter 2 – The Normans make their mark

After their success at Hastings in 1066 the Normans wasted little time in getting to grips with the wealthier parts of their new country. The Domesday Book, compiled less than 20 years after the invasion, shows this area to be wealthy and comparatively well populated. Brome, Oakley, Hoxne and Eye are all shown to be among the largest 20 per cent of settlements recorded in Domesday. Oakley was larger than Brome and is recorded as having one mill.

The area was part directly owned by King William with other lands owned by various barons, including Robert Malet, Roger Bigod and Ralph of Beaufour. Some lands were also owned by the Abbey at Bury St Edmunds and Thetford Priory.

Near Church Farm is a moat around an island with buried ruins which is a dedicated ancient monument. Little is known of what is there and still be discovered and researched, but it could have been the home of D'Aviller who came to England with William the Conqueror. Similar names which may have shared D'Aviller as their original root are found as field names close by.

Our family's real exposure to the highest levels of Norman lordships came in 1956, when my grandfather bought Abbey Farm in Eye for my brother Michael. At that time it was a working farm. Centuries of records were stored there, with a history going back to another of William's companions, William Malet, or *Guillaume Malet de Graville* to give him his French title.

This knight is featured on the Bayeaux tapestry, on horseback with a hawk in hand. As a close companion of the king Malet was given vast lands in Yorkshire and East Anglia; his was the largest single lordship in East Anglia. He was appointed high sheriff of Suffolk and Norfolk in 1070 and made Eye his regional capital.

Eye Abbey

William Malet died in 1071 and was succeeded by his son Robert Malet. He established a Benedictine Abbey in Eye in 1080 dedicated to his father. Eye Abbey was modelled on Bernay Abbey in Normandy, which still stands. The priors were appointed in France and dues were paid to Bernay.

Eye Priory grew to become an extraordinarily wealthy church. It drew allegiance, and dues, from a large number of subsidiary local churches as far afield as Badingham, Brundish, Laxfield, Playford, Tattingstone and Wingfield. It also owned large parts of Dunwich and received payments from what was at the time one of East Anglia's wealthiest ports, until the sea took it in the 14th century.

Queen Anne, wife of Richard II from 1382 until her death in 1394, became Lord of the Honour of Eye. By this time Norman England had become Anglicised. She sent the French Monks of Eye Priory back to France. It became English and it is believed this was when the building west of Abbey Farmhouse was built, although its exact original purpose is not clear.

It later contained a Bake House and a Brew House. The first floor became living quarters. Queen Mary, sister of Henry VIII and widow the French King Louis, married Charles Brandon, Duke of Suffolk is 1515. As Lord of the Honour of Eye she installed, at the southern end of the first floor, an office for the steward and bailiffs. This chamber is also known as the Queen's Chamber.

Henry VIII's 1534 Act of Supremacy led to the dissolution of the monasteries and Eye Priory was given to Brandon. The assets were stripped and the church buildings were either re-purposed or collapsed. The Priors Lodging, which was attached to the church, survived and is now called The Abbey. The brick façade hides a medieval stone and timbered building.

It was probably because the stewards' and bailiffs' offices were separate from the main priory that their records weren't touched when the foot soldiers of the dissolution came looking for precious items and relics they could sell.

When Abbey Farm was bought by my grandfather in 1956 the farm office had not been touched since 1921. My brother witnessed archive staff from Suffolk County Council examining documents, many of them old priory records. They took items of interest back to Ipswich and said the rest could be disposed of. I spent two evenings looking through then and found items that referred to my family and I also gained a lot of details about the Kerrison era.

There was also a pile of documents that were very old and in Latin stored from the Priory. I did not look thoroughly through these papers. I had no knowledge of the Red Book of Eye at the time. The Red Book could possibly have been in the pile and was burnt with the rest of the debris.

The Red Book of Eye

The Red Book of Eye is now presumed lost but was originally a collection of extracts from the Gospels belonging to St Felix of Dunwich. He was the first Christian bishop of the Eastern Angles, appointed in the late 600s. The book has several antiquarian references and could have been removed to Eye Priory when Dunwich eroded into the sea. It was called the Red Book although some reports say it was reputedly coloured purple, a rare and exclusive pigment in those days.

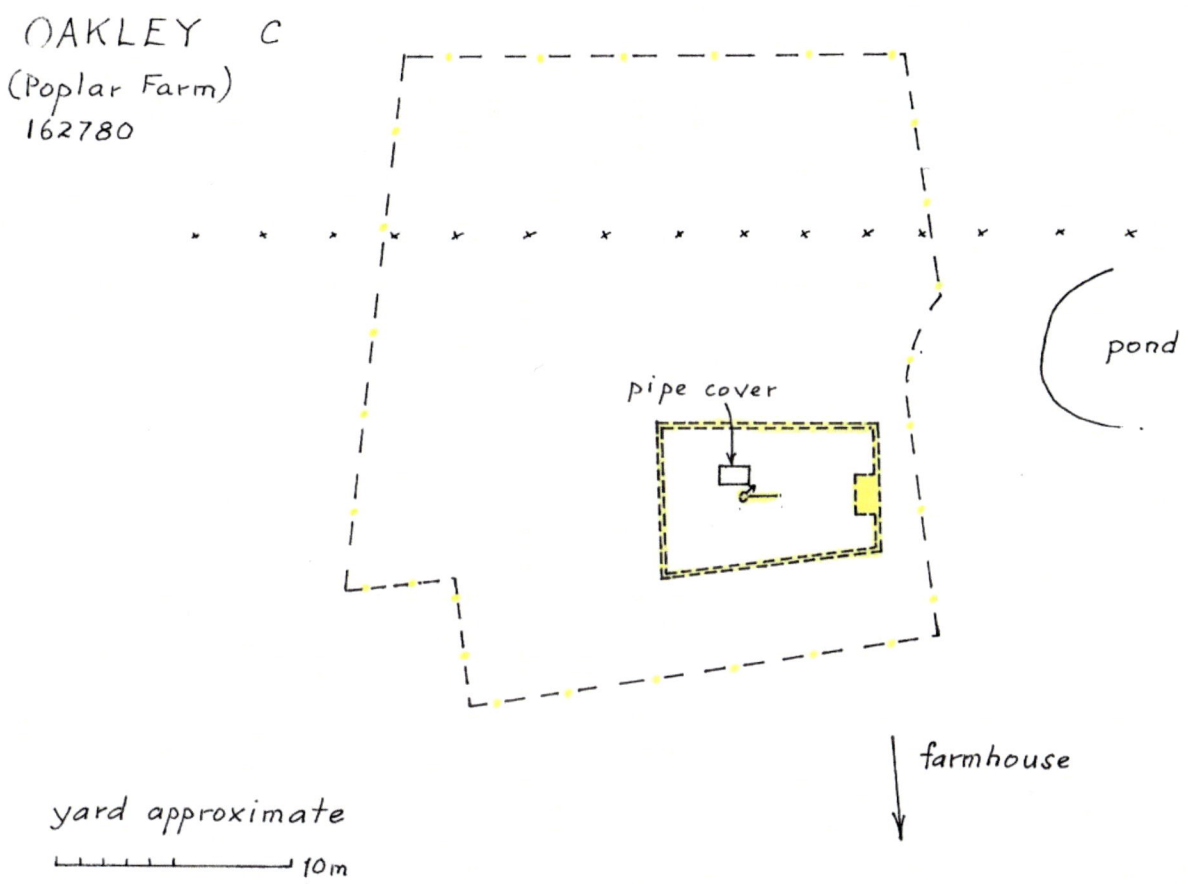

The site of a Saxon Church near Poplar Farm, Lower Oakley, was discovered following excavations by Doctors David and Bridget Trump in the 1970s. Dr David Trump was a leading archeologist at Pembroke College Cambridge and an early advocate of the science of carbon dating in archeology.

OAKLEY St Andrew
(Alder Carr 153782)

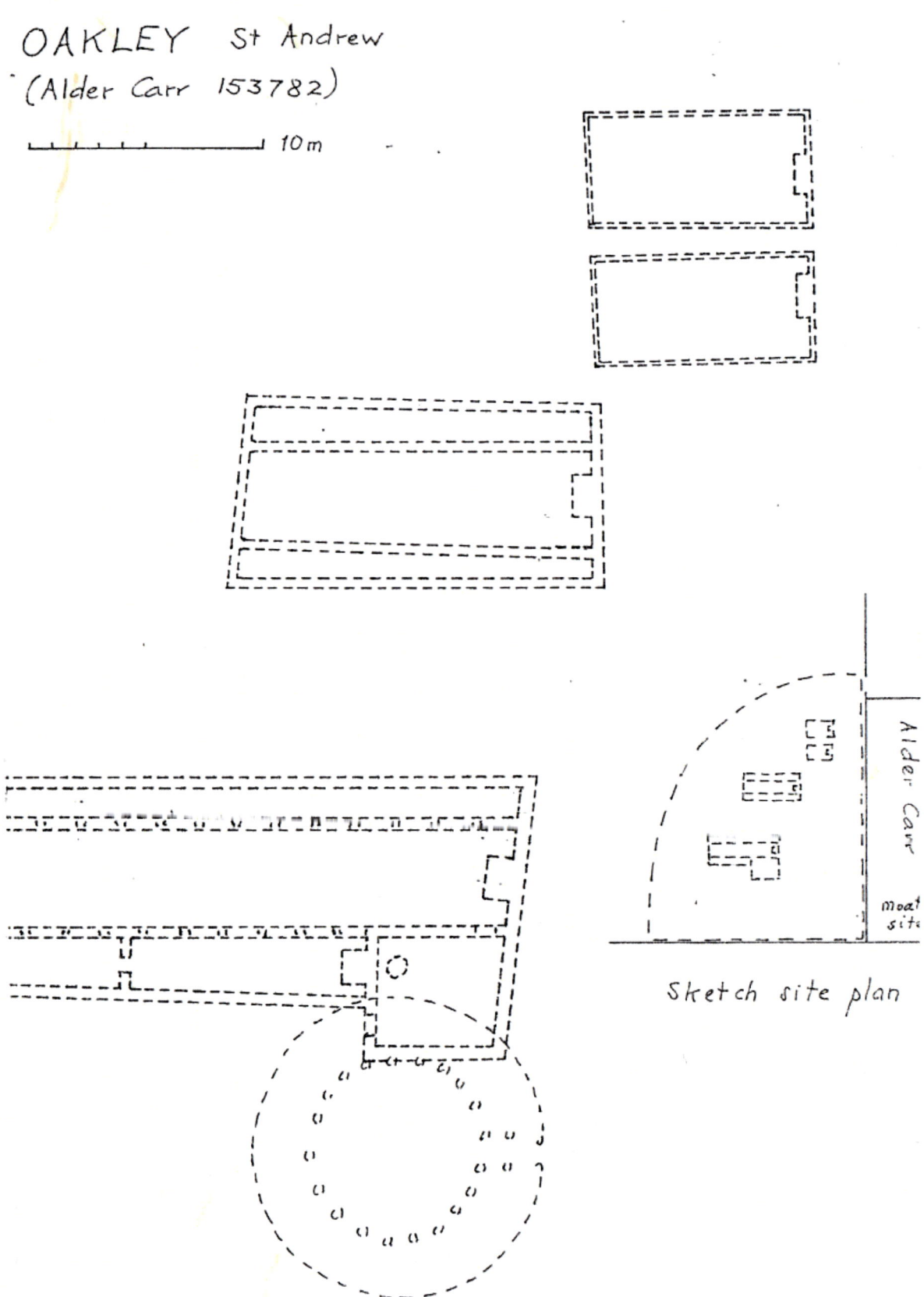

Sketch site plan

A second Saxon site was identified by the Trumps close to Alder Carr, near the River Waveney. This also incuded evidence of a Saxon church.

Artefacts found during excavation work on a moat near Church Farm, Brome. Evidence dated it to Saxon times. Indications of several nearby buildings occupied in the 12th century were also recorded. A second moat with ruins on the island dates to the Norman period. It is a designated ancient monument though yet to be fully researched.

Field plan near the confluence of the Dove and the Waveney, showing 'doles' - raised stretches of ground from medieval strip farming. The practice continued into Norman times but their physical layout was worthy of note in this 1838 tithe map of the area.

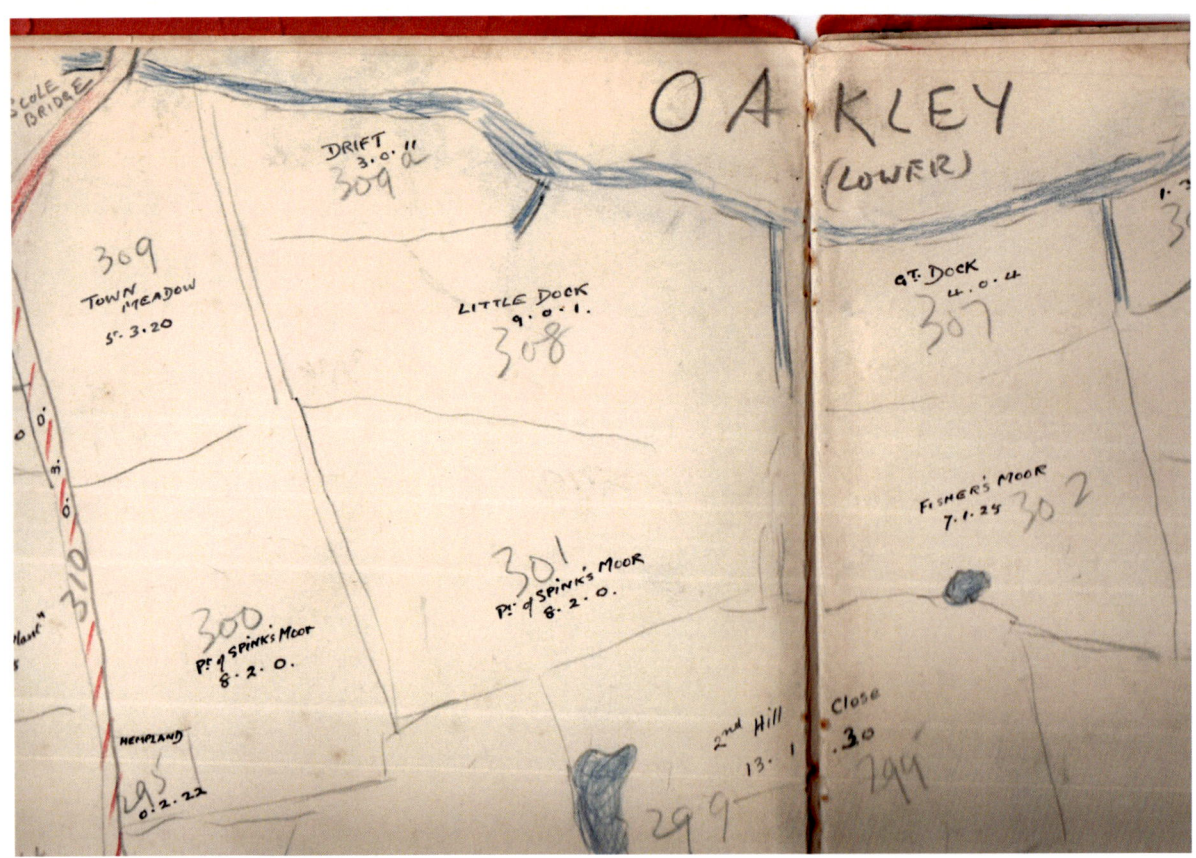

Old field names often provide useful clues about the history of a place. This illustration from a Brome and Oakley tithe map of 1838 shows the field names of Warren Hill farm as they border the River Waveney eastwards from the old Scole Bridge. In the 1950s the author witnessed work on this stretch of river where very old bankside timbers were being dredged out along Dock meadows. The implication is that these were old docking facilities at the head of navigation of the Waveney, possibly dating back to Saxon times and perhaps even Roman.

Chapter 3 – The Era of the Estates

The Normans set the pattern for large landed estates for its privileged classes. By the 15th century the open field systems and common lands gave way to large tracts of privately owned land which in turn became some of the great estates of England. They made agriculture more efficient and productive, bestowing wealth and privilege on the families who owned them, though the peasantry suffered.

One family came to dominate Brome and Oakley during this period. The Cornwallis family rose to operate at the highest levels of society and wrote their names into world history. But in the 1400s they began quietly enough. Ling Manor, on the border of Brome and Oakley, was owned by the Bucton family. Their daughter Philippa married John Cornwallis who built up the estate and an early version of Brome Hall.

The Cornwallis family went on to expand the estate and over several generations took their place in Parliament and gave high service to their monarch, country and empire. They prospered during the turbulent 1500s, a period of great change in English history when the Tudors reigned. Sir John's son, Thomas Cornwallis re-built Brome Hall. It was reputed to be the second largest hall in Suffolk. He had previously (1552-53) been Sheriff of Norfolk and Suffolk and a member of Parliament for Suffolk, positions which required he maintain some trappings of status.

It also thrust him into the front line when Robert Kett's rebellion attracted popular support against the enclosures movement. In 1549 some 16,000 rebels gathered on Mousehold Heath in Norwich and Cornwallis was one of the leaders of the Marquess of Northampton's army sent to quell the uprising. Their first efforts failed and Cornwallis was captured, though released later when a larger force defeated the rebels.

The reformation

Sir Thomas was also a high profile figure during the turbulent transition from catholic Queen Mary to the protestant Queen Elizabeth. As a staunch catholic he proclaimed for Mary at Framlingham castle and his support for her led to his appointment as Treasurer of the port of Calais, then an English possession. However Calais was lost back to the French under his jurisdiction. That, and his support for Mary, meant he retired from public life when Elizabeth became queen. His monument, with his wife Lady Anne, is a notable feature in St Mary's Brome.

Whether he was responsible for the loss of Calais or the victim of circumstances is not clear. But shortly afterwards a singing game was circulating which went:

Who built Brome Hall?
Sir Thomas Cornwallis.
How did he build it?
By the selling of Calais.

What got ye for Calais
Sir Thomas Cornwallis?
Brome Hall, Brome Hall
As big as a Palace.

The Boke of Brome

Whereas the Red Book of Eye is presumed lost The Boke of Brome still exists and is to be found in Yale University Beinecke Rare Books Library. Written in the late 15th century and early 16th by two hands the first section is a 'Commonplace' book of devotional chapters presumed written by a religious scribe, though unknown. The second section comprises more day-to-day writings and accounts by one Robert Melton, a farmer of Stuston. It is considered an important late Medieval work.

The book found its way into Brome Hall where it was translated by Lady Caroline Kerrison sometime in the mid 1800s. From there it remained out of public sight until the 20th century when international interest in ancient British artefacts was high.

It was re-discovered by an American academic Richard Leighton Greene during a visit to Oakley House, then occupied by Mrs Douglas Hamilton, daughter of Lady Bateman of Brome Hall. He presumably recognised its importance and interest in it grew in US academic circles. When it subsequently came up for auction, despite efforts to keep it in the UK, Yale University bought it. However it can be viewed online in its entirety.

Sir Thomas was well connected with the Royal court and his descendants could expect to follow his example. The name Cornwallis appears regularly whenever the royal house needed support. They fought with both Charles I and II and represented England in Spain during the period of the inquisition.

English martyr

The Cornwallis family were clearly politically astute, negotiating the Catholic – Protestant Reformation to retain their position in society. Their wealth helped, enabling them to become recusants, i.e. allowed to continue as practising Catholics for a fee. But others were less inclined to bend or pay up. Henry Morse was was born in Brome in 1593. His parents were Robert and Margaret Morse of Tivetshall St Mary. Margaret's parents were the Collinsons of Brome, to where she returned to have her children.

Young Henry studied for the Catholic priesthood in France and Rome. He rose to prominence as a Jesuit priest in what was now a largely Protestant England and ministered selflessly to the sick and dying during the great plague of the 1630s. Despite the anti-Catholic feeling in the country at the time he refused to renounce his faith. For this he was hanged, drawn and quartered at Tyburn, London, in 1645. He was canonised in 1929 and named as one of the Forty English Martyrs in 1970.

Meanwhile the Cornwallis family continued to prosper and in the 1700s took a place on the world stage. Two brothers, Charles and William (b. 1738 and 1744) served the crown in various world skirmishes, including the Napoleonic Wars, the American War of Independence and in India - key influencers on the shape and reach of the British Empire. William was a career Navy man who rose to become Commander of the Channel Fleet at the time of the Battle of Trafalgar. Had Nelson lost at Trafalgar William's Channel Fleet was the last line of defence against a French invasion.

Military experience and parliamentary loyalty to the monarch encouraged George III to appoint Charles Cornwallis to lead a force of reinforcements to the British Army already fighting in the American War of Independence. That history is well known; Cornwallis surrendered to George Washington at the Battle of Yorktown in October 1781 and America secured the independence it had declared in 1776.

After that defeat the county of Brome was created in Canada to house the British Army before returning to England. However, Charles also established the border between the US and Canada later ratified in the Treaty of Paris. That success may have softened the blow as on his return to England he received the title of Marquis and was appointed Governor of India where he is considered to have done quite well.

Not all the Cornwallis family were military men. Frederick Cornwallis, Charles's uncle, was Archbishop of Canterbury from 1768 – 83. Clearly there was some piety amongst the family, the most prominent evidence today being the Almshouses, formally the Almshouses of Elizabeth, Lady Cornwallis, opposite the gates of the family seat, Brome Hall.

Brome Hall

Brome Hall ceased to be the main seat of the Cornwallis family when Charles Cornwallis family moved into Culford Hall, near Bury St Edmunds, during the 18th century. Culford Hall was a 16th century hall originally built by Sir Nathaniel Bacon and heavily renovated by Charles Cornwallis in the 1790s.

Only some parts of the old Brome Hall survive. The buildings to the left of the modern Hall, originally stables, include an old clock tower – the clock port is still clearly visible. The original turret clock was made in the 1680s by Thomas Tompion, described as the `Father of English Clockmaking'. It is today considered unique and after being in the possession of the British Museum is now thought to be in the USA. It appeared in several auction catalogues between 1982 and 2013.

That clock would have seen the end of 400 years of continuous Cornwallis history in Brome when, in 1823, the Brome and Oakley Estate was sold to Sir Edward Kerrison for £80,000. Sir Edward, a renown soldier who had fought at Waterloo, was the son of Mathias Kerrison of Oakley Park, and so the two the two neighbouring estates were joined.

The Kerrison estate became famous for its shooting, hunting, hare coursing and otter hunting. The playboy Prince of Wales, later King Edward VII, was amongst its famous visitors, sometimes with Mrs Alice Keppel in attendance, one of Prince 'Bertie's' admirers. Alice Keppel is the great grandmother of Queen Camilla while King Charles is the great great grandson of Edward VII.

Sir Edward Kerrison's son, Sir Edward Clarence Kerrison, also made his mark outside the estate. He part financed Eye Town Hall and built the Kerrison school in Thorndon, today converted to houses, modernised St Mary's Brome and supported a branch line of the Great Eastern Railway from Yaxley to Eye. A monument to his life and work stands in Eye market square.

Estate records

After my grandfather purchased Eye Abbey and the farm we also discovered the Estates records which had been virtually untouched since the sale of the estate in the 1920s. The records covered the period of the Kerrisons' era going back to the 19th century. Most of the papers went to the Ipswich Museum. From these records it is possible to get a picture of village life in that era. A hundred years before the estate owned more than 7,000 acres spread over 12 villages, and consisted of 288 houses, 38 farms, and many small-holdings and tenanted allotments. In Brome and Oakley 88 houses were owned by the Kerrison estate. The only Brome farm which was not part of the Kerrison estate was Parke Farm – their family had been owner occupiers for 200 years.

The average wage for estate workers was around £2 per week. This included carpenters, bricklayers, wood men and general workers. Winter hours were 6:30am to 5pm with mealtimes of 1 hour. During the summer an extra half an hour was worked. On Mondays work did not start until 7am and Saturday work finished at 4pm.

Income for the estate came from rents for houses and farms. Tenant farmers were paying an average rent of just over £1 per acre per annum. This included their house and farm cottages. Other tenant cottages were averaging about £4 per annum rent, most were paying a further ten shillings (50p) for allotments.

Agnes Burrell, Baroness Bateman, lived in Brome Hall after the death of her brother, Sir Edward Kerrison in 1886. His main residence was by then Oakley Park, and he only resided at Brome Hall occasionally.

Renting the Park during this time were the Hill-Wood Family, connected by marriage to the Kerrisons. Three generations of Hill-Woods were directors and chairmen of Arsenal Football Club. The rent for Oakley Park was £1000 per annum. They also employed 3 gardeners and 10 gamekeepers as well as the domestic staff. The Park house was just east of Oakley, in Hoxne, and the Park itself was in both parishes.

Farming went into decline around the time of Sir Edward Kerrison's death. The estate was managed by trustees for his youngest daughter, Lady Agnes Bateman, and accounts seemed to indicate that outgoings exceeded income. She died in the spring of 1918 when, after 400 years, the fortunes of this great estate had sunk low. The post-war slump meant that unemployment was rife and farm workers' wages were reduced to 26 shillings (£1.30) per week.

The trustees of the Brome and Oakley Estate decided to sell the Oakley Park Estate of over 6000 acres as well as over 200 Hoxne and Eye houses. Sir Rowland Hodge purchased Oakley Park Estate as an investment. But in 1918 the price of land plummeted and Hodge was unable to finance the purchase and the assets, with Brome Hall, were put into public administration.

Sir Thomas Tacon from Eye had an outstanding loan against the estate and offered to purchase the remaining Brome Estate. The Administrators cancelled the Hodge sale and installed Sir Thomas's daughter Maude as tenant. Unfortunately, Sir Thomas died before completion in 1921 and it was 1924 before the sale was completed by his executors.

The last years

Between the wars local man Alfred King was caretaker of Brome Hall. Maude Tacon was on the south coast when the army turned up in 1940 and requisitioned the Hall. He was given 48 hours to clear the rooms for army occupation and with a gang of labourers he succeeded. Dunkirk was being evacuated and within a week the house and gardens were full of troops. The Hall and Brome Avenue became an army base with military vehicles, Bren gun carriers and army supplies and munitions. The Eye entrance was demolished to allow tanks and their carriers to gain access.

In 1944 the military left the estate for the Normandy landings and the Hall fell into disrepair. The house and its remaining acreage was bought by the Wests in 1953. Despite some interest in keeping the house habitable there were, in those days, no grants for such work and in 1962 the much decayed building was demolished to be replaced by a modern hall completed in 1964.

FIG. 14. Brome in 1726; redrawn from the map in the Ipswich and East Suffolk
H A 66: 484/753.

An early map of Brome showing Ivy House and Brome Hall at the top, the junction with Buck Lane in the middle and St Mary's Brome near the bottom.

The Priory of St. Peter, Eye

An artistic impression of Eye Priory which was founded by Robert Malet in the 1080s. It is modeled on Bernay Abbey in Normandy. Robert Malet was the son of William Malet, one of William the Conqueror's knights. The priory was suppressed in February 1537. The smaller building on the left, part of which survives today as Abbey House, was built around 1500.

William Malet came to England with William the Conqueror in 1066. For his services to the king he was granted 75,000 acres in Suffolk and the position of Lord of the Honour of Eye. He built Eye Castle while his son Robert built Eye Priory. The family resided in Eye deer park, one of the largest in Suffolk, and his manor could have been on the site of what is now Park Farm, between Eye and Thorndon. At the time of the sale of Brome and Oakley estate the Flowerdew family were tenants of the nearby Clint and Park farms. They paid £280 for 300 acres. Count von Jacobs of Oakley House was paying £1000 for the shooting rights.

The tomb of Sir Thomas Cornwallis and his wife, Anne, in Brome Church. They lie next to similar tombs of his father Sir John Cornwallis and his wife Mary.

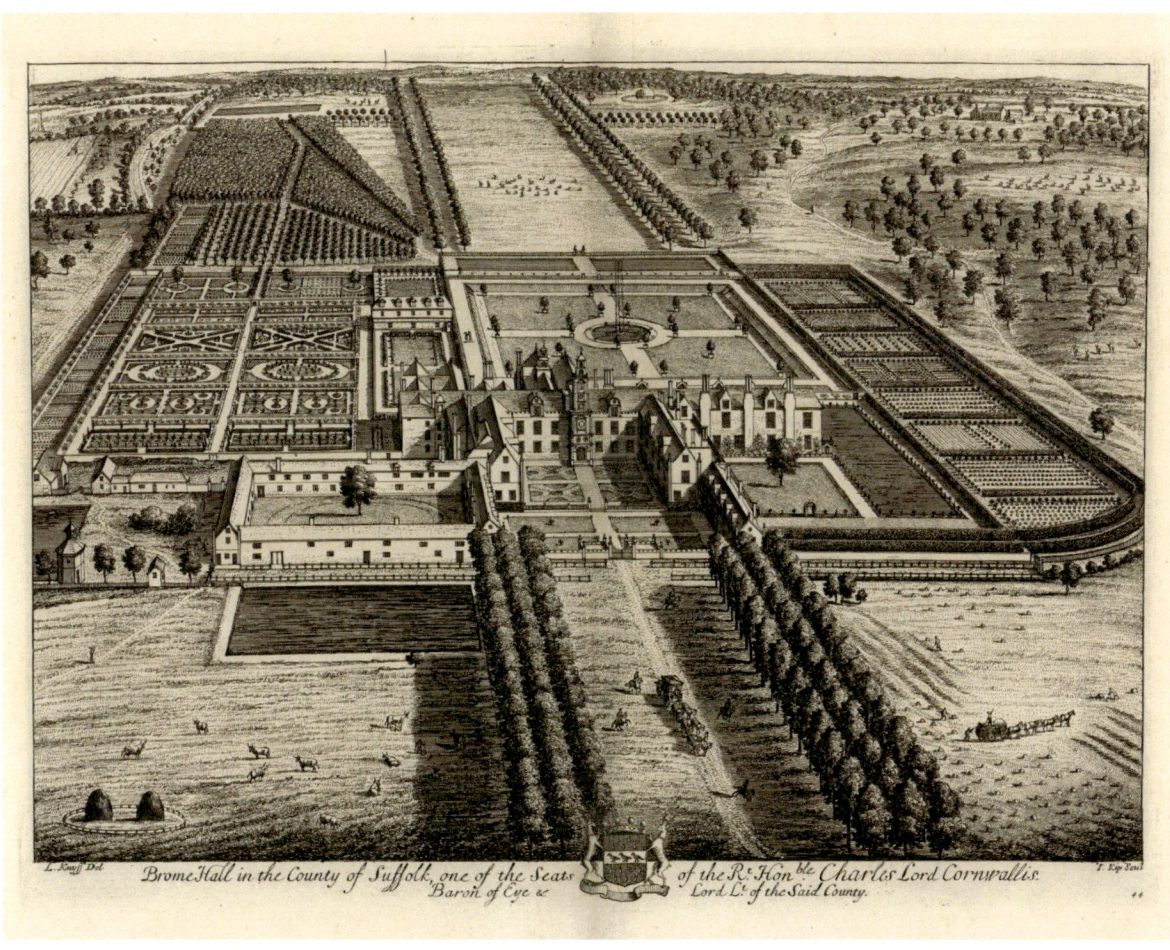

An early print of Brome Hall and its famous formal gardens from around 1700. Only parts of the stable block on the left now survive.

A later view of Brome Hall, possibly early Victorian, showing the clock tower above the stables on the right.

Oakley Park House, home of the Kerrison family. General Sir Edward Kerrison also bought Brome Hall estate and amalgamated the two into a major sporting and farming estate.

Portrait of Charles Cornwallis, who surrendered to George Washington at the Battle of Yorktown in 1781, thus securing independence for America. Cornwallis was made a Marquis in 1786 and appointed Governor of India by George III. He was born in Brome Hall in 1738 but lived his later life in Culford Hall, near Bury St Edmunds.

Oakley Park House was near Hoxne and, though demolished in 1926 is survived by its stables, now converted to a private house. It was at the centre of a large and highly regarded sporting estate, attracting aristocratic parties. The estate was broken up and sold in 1920.

A hunt meet in front of Oakley Park House early 1900s.

A plan of part of Oakley Park estate prepared for the 1920 land sale. This section shows how the estate straddled the river Dove into Oakley and Hoxne. Hoxne village is shown at the lower right hand corner with Billingford bridge top left.

By direction of Rowland Frederic William Hodge, Esq.

Particulars and Plan

OF THE

BEAUTIFUL RESIDENTIAL & SPORTING ESTATE

OF

OAKLEY PARK

SITUATE IN THE

PARISHES OF EYE, OCCOLD, BRAISEWORTH, THRANDESTON, YAXLEY, BROME, OAKLEY, STUSTON, HOXNE, DENHAM, BILLINGFORD AND HORHAM

IN THE

COUNTIES OF SUFFOLK AND NORFOLK

THE ESTATE IS SITUATED ABOUT HALFWAY BETWEEN THE IMPORTANT TOWNS OF IPSWICH AND NORWICH, ABOUT 3 HOURS FROM LONDON, AND 5 MILES FROM MELLIS STATION, ON THE G. E. MAIN LINE RAILWAY, WHERE EXPRESS TRAINS STOP

To be Sold by Auction as a Whole or in Lots

(Unless previously Sold by Private Treaty)

BY

CASTIGLIONE & SCOTT

IN THE

GREAT WHITE HORSE HOTEL, IPSWICH, ON TUESDAY, THE 18TH DAY OF MAY 1920, AT 2 O' CLOCK PROMPT

A poster advertises the May 1920 sale of Oakley Park estate. Its extraordinary size is illustrated by the detail of the number of parishes in the area it occupied.

Top, Early photo of Ivy House and, bottom, one of its younger, earlier occupants, Arthur Flowerdew, painted in the 1840s. A seven-year old having his portrait painted indicates a well-to-do family, abeit he was the eldest son. In later life Arthur took over Billingford Hall and was the father of Victoria Cross hero Gordon Flowerdew.

A photograph of Church Farm, Brome, taken by the noted pioneer Victorian era photographer Cleer Alger, who was born and lived in Diss.

Top, One of the rare photographs of the 19th century Brome Hall, taken the year of the estate sale. It shows the south facade and formal gardens. Bottom, The picture shows Alfred King winding the rare Thomas Tompion turret clock in Brome Hall clock tower still working in 1939. It would have been made in the 1600s. It was auctioned in London in 2013 for over £70,000. Alfred King was caretaker of Brome Hall and was present in 1940 when the army requisitioned the Hall and grounds for Dunkirk evacuees.

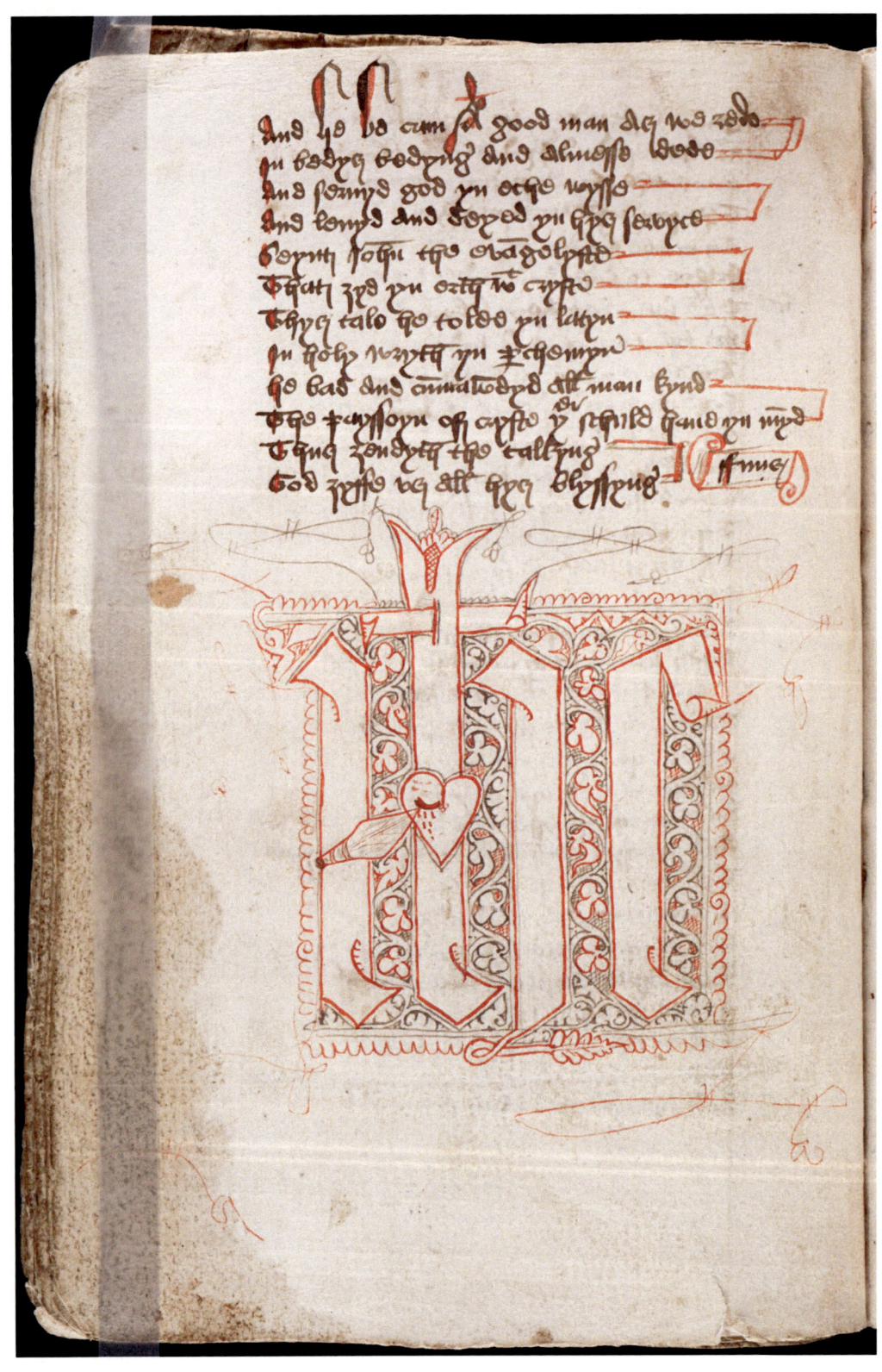

An illustrated page from the earlier part of The Boke of Brome, comprising religious texts written by an unknown scribe in the late 1400s. The later part comprises secular notes thought to have been written in the early 1500s by Stuston farmer Robert Melton. It passed to Brome Hall and was rediscovered in Oakley House in the 1960s. It is now in the Beinecke Collection of Yale University Library.

OAKLEY HOUSE COACHMAN AND CARRIAGE

The Chestnuts Oakley

Top, Mrs Douglas Hamilton's coachman and carriage outside Chestnuts, Oakley. Hon Mrs Douglas Hamilton, Lady Bateman's daughter, owned Oakley House, the Park and Farm. Bottom, Mrs von Jakobs, a Lithuanian Countess outside Oakley House in 1900.

Chapter 4 – A Time of Change

The misfortunes of the 'big house' which dominated the locality were not isolated from broader social changes. The period leading up to WW1 was also the culmination of 150 years of enormous changes in agriculture and industry. But while the factories were turning the towns and cities into a mechanised economy Brome and Oakley were still dominated by local farming.

Men and horses from the two villages did the work. There was a water mill on the River Dove and a windmill further up. Blacksmiths' forges serviced the horses, forged tools and repaired ironwork. Village shops catered for families and there were public houses in both Brome and Oakley. The Swan on the A140 closed only recently while The Buck, now No. 1-2 The Street, opposite the village hall, closed many years ago. Oakley Green Man is now Green Man house, near the telephone box in Lower Oakley. Drinking water in Brome was sourced from the well, now capped near the village sign in front of the Almshouses. Children went to the school in the village until 1969, when it was closed and they transferred to Eye. Today the old school is the 'new' village hall and centre of community activities. In the 2020s there are still several people living in the village and attending village hall events who were pupils in the old school.

The previous village hall was on a site now occupied by Buck Lane House. It was built in 1924 using sections of two old railway carriages which were reconstructed into one building. The carriages came from the West engineering factory in Diss. How they got from Diss to Brome in those days must have been quite a sight! Once the new hall was up and running the old hall was used for several years to shelter cattle until it was demolished in the late 1990s.

At the beginning of the 1900s Brome and Oakley weren't done with writing a place in world history. Two world wars still had to be fought and won. And the first one would produce a headline-grabbing local hero.

Local hero

During WW1 Oakley Park because a training ground for mounted regiments. The first to arrive came from Alberta, Canada, with 500 horses from the Strathcona Horse regiment. Training on the Park must have felt like home ground for one of its officers, Lieutenant Gordon Flowerdew, who was originally born in Billingford Hall in 1885 and emigrated to Canada in 1903.

Lt Flowerdew already had a reputation for dashing bravery when in 1918 he led one of the last cavalry charges of WW1 against a much superior force of German infantry at Moreuil Wood, in the Somme. He was wounded in action and died shortly after. He was posthumously awarded the Victoria Cross, the highest military honour, 'For conspicuous bravery'.

The action was painted by Sir Alfred Munnings, a Mendham boy, who was one of the official war artists. The charge was also commemorated in 2018 with a reconstruction, featuring George West of Warren Hill farm.

The Flowerdews are an established local dynasty. One branch of the family occupied Ivy House in the 1800s. The 1841 census records its residents as:

- John Flowerdew
- Emily Flowerdew nee Bloomfield
- Arthur Flowerdew age 7
- Edgar Flowerdew age 5
- Charles Flowerdew age 2
- Jane Snape – governess
- Mary Lockett – female servant
- Emily Wormer – female servant
- Dinah Wilby – widow
- John Howlett – male servant.

The fact that young Arthur had his portrait painted aged seven indicates a well-to-do family.

During 1928-58 Ivy house was the home of Mr Charles A West (the author's grandfather) and his wife, and daughter Ruth, who subsequently married Jack Prior, county councillor for North Hartismere. Jack and Ruth continued living at Ivy House and farmed Peck's Farm.

Mechanisation

The period between the two world wars saw big changes in agriculture, still the lifeblood of Brome and Oakley. The loss of a generation of able bodied men across the country together with the mechanisation developed during WWI saw the beginning of the end of horse and man power. Machines began to take over.

In the 1930s there were ten farms in the two villages and most of them employed villagers as labour. Wests' farms had tractors early on, alongside the horses. Charles West had begun selling tractors from his garages in Diss during WWI and through the 1920s. He changed his steam engine for a tracked tractor in 1936 and had a German-invented straw baler to go behind a threshing machine. Alex Lewis was the first farmer in the area to have a combine harvester.

At this time nearly every farm had a dairy herd, pigs and poultry. Some also kept sheep. Today it is heavily arable, which has seen the old, small fields with hedges opened up into large tracts of land suitable for big machines.

Schooldays

Village children went to school in the village. The school, like many others, was run by the Church of England, with Brome coming under the Diocese of St Edmundsbury. Between 30 and 40 children attended with Oakley children walking the mile or more there and back every day. This routine continued throughout 1939-45. Villager Gordon Elliott remembers when children caught between home and school when an air raid warning was sounded were supposed to run home or to school, whichever was nearer. Needless to say very few ran towards school!

The school closed its doors in 1969 and pupils were transferred to Eye. The building was then bought by the Parish Council for community use, replacing the old railway carriage sheds at the top of Buck Lane which had served as the village hall since 1924. A prodigious effort of fund-raising and practical work saw the village hall open as a community centre in 1971.

Elsewhere in the villages modernisation was moving only slowly. There were fewer than ten cars in pre-1939 Brome and Oakley. Grid electricity reached the villages in 1939 while mains water was not laid on until the 1950s and mains drainage not until the 1960s.

The old village hall was built in the 1920s and made up of two old railway carriages opened up and covered by the apex roof. The carriage windows are visible as is the roof outline of the carriages in the gable. It was used as a cattle and storage shed after the old village school became the new village hall in 1971. It stood on the corner of Buck Lane until it was demolished in the 1990s to make way for Buck Lane House.

The old school in Brome Street, date unknown but presumed pre-1938, showing School House on the left and the old Post Office on the right. The school closed its doors in 1969 and formally reopened as the village hall in 1971.

King Edward VII's visit to Quidenham, October 1909.
Back Row, L to R: Viscount Bury, Hon. Col. George Keppel, Canon Edward Garnier, Sir George Halford, ?, ?.
Middle Row, L to R: Earl of Derby, Lord Haldane, Earl of Albemarle, Earl of Leicester (Lord Lt. of Norfolk).
Front Row, L to R: Lady Chelsea, Viscountess Bury, Countess of Albemarle, King Edward VII, Countess of Leicester, Hon. Mrs. George Keppel, Lady Elizabeth Keppel.

The grand houses of England, including Brome Hall and Oakley Park, often hosted aristocratic house parties. This photo is of such a group at Quidenham Hall in 1909, owned then by the Keppel family. It shows King Edward VII sitting next but one to Mrs George Keppel, in the striped coat, described as one of his favourite mistresses. Similar parties took place at Brome Hall and Oakley Park. Alice Keppel is the great grandmother of Queen Camilla while Edward VII's great great grandson is King Charles III. Quidenham Hall is now a Carmelite monastery. Between the wars the Wests rented 1000 acres of the Quidenham Estate from Mrs Keppel.

Top The original rectory in Brome was near St Mary's, Brome, close to Church Farm. It is now demolished. The rectory pictured above is now The Oaksmere. Previously it was the Dower House for Brome Hall estate. Bottom, Rev. Cory Elvin was last Rector to reside in the Rectory at Brome, pictured in 1939. There was also a curate in the parish; The Old Curacy is opposite the rear gates of the Oaksmere.

Lt Gordon Flowerdew, pictured above inspecting his troop on Brome Park before embarking for France during WW1.

Alfred Munnings' painting of the cavalry charge at Moreuil Wood in March 1918 led by Lt Gordon Flowerdew of the Strathcona Horse. Flowerdew was born in Billingford and emigrated to Canada as a young man, only to return with his regiment to Brome and Oakley for training before leaving for the Somme. He died after this action and was awarded the Victoria Cross 'for conspicuous bravery'. The painting is now in the Canadian War Museum.

The blacksmith's in Billingford in 1915 shoeing horses from the Strathcona Horse regiment stationed on Oakley Park. The building is now a private house in the row facing the windmill.

In WW1 almost one million horses were drafted into military service in France, half of which were with the British Army. Hay, straw and feed were required in huge quantities and was exported from England. Charles Augustus West (standing in front of tractor) had a contract to supply one train load a week of hay and straw which went from Diss Station. The War Department supplied the baling machine, marked WD in the picture.

After WW1 the agricultural machinery business took off. Charles Augustus West and William Chitty together formed an engineering and foundry business in Diss which in the 1920s became the local agents for Rolls Royce, until 1923, and Ford Tractors. This picture shows their supplier's badge. Their works was on the site now occupied by Morrisons supermarket.

The 'back gate' to Brome Hall estate near the present day Bowls Club on the outskirts of Eye. The brickwork was demolished early in WW2 to allow tanks and heavy vehicles to pass through. These then lay camouflaged under the woods of the estate.

Drilling and harrowing on a local farm, with some fine Suffolk punches doing the heavy work.

Horse power started to give way to mechanised kit in the 1930s. Here an early Allis Chalmers tractor clears sugar beet rows and lifts potatoes in 1938.

1938 First Combine Harvester in District GA Lewis's Farm

Also in 1938 the first combine harvester appeared in Brome and Oakley (top). The lower, later, photo shows pea harvesters at work; the peas were transported to the Birds Eye processing plant near Lowestoft.

Earth moving used to be a very labour intensive business. This photo shows men and horses and carts in the early 1900s moving gravel to make hard standing around Hoxne Church. Hoxne village is in the background.

Farm workers with 40 years or more service would be presented with medals at the annual farm dinner. This C A West & Son dinner took place in 1980 at the White Lion Inn in Eye, with John Gummer, M.P. for Eye and J R. Vipond of the Royal Agricultural Society as guests. The White Lion was a coaching inn until 1840. It closed in 1986. The author is seated, middle row, third from right.

Food HALL

By 1944 Brome airfield was fully functional with 490 Bomb Group on station. At its peak over 2500 men were quartered in the parish. The control tower pictured above was sited at the Brome end of the main runway. The food hall was off Nicks Lane.

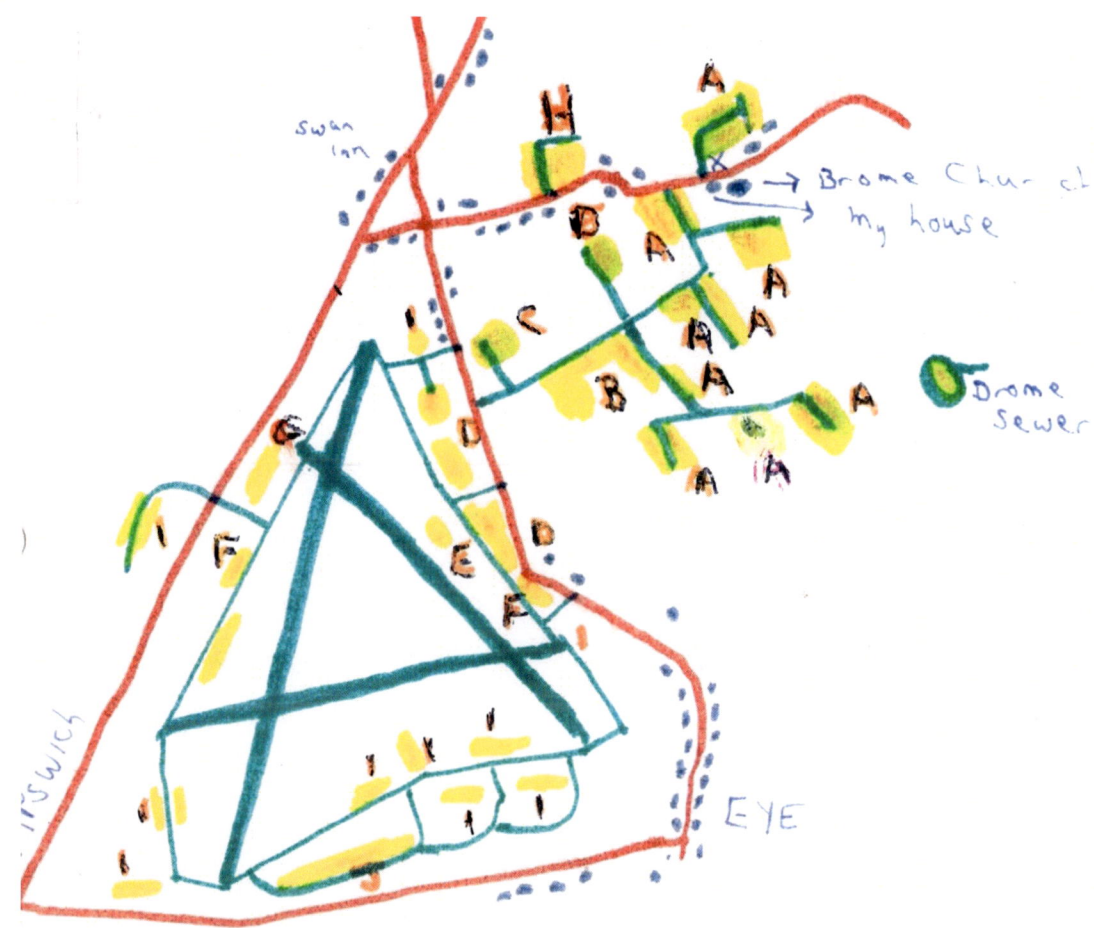

——	Public Roads
——	Airfield constructed roads
▮	Runways
A	Area under concrete and Nissen HutsLiving Quarters
B	Feeding and Recreation
C	Control Centre HQ
D	Storage and Repair Depots
E	Control Tower
F	Aircraft Hangers
G	Firing Range
H	Hospital
I	Aircraft Dispersal
J	Bomb Store

This hand drawn map of Eye Airfield by Peter West shows the original runway layout and the extent to which the airmen and support staff on the airfield occupied Brome village.

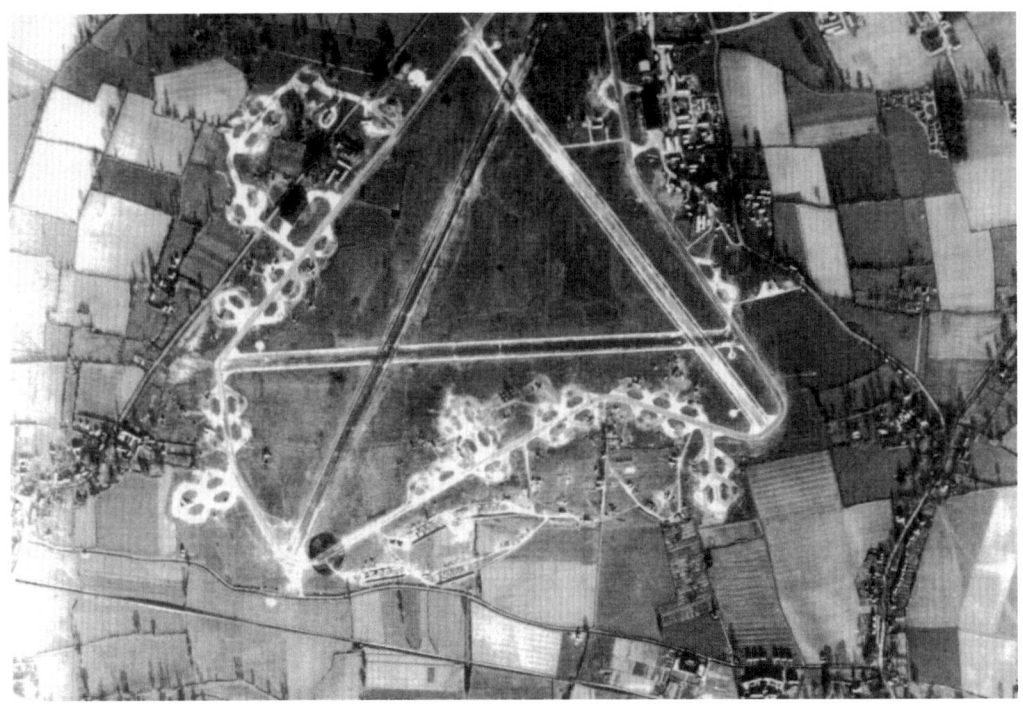

Aerial view of Eye Airfield showing the runways, some perimeter buildings and parking bays. The semi-circle of parking bays cut through by the A140 is top left. When planes were moved on and off this section traffic on the A140 was stopped.

In 1944 two Flying Fortresses from Cambridgeshire collided in mid-air near Eye. Only three airmen out of a combined crew of 20 survived. The planes broke up on impact and debris and bombs were scattered over a wide area, scarring the landscape and destroying Church Farm's cattle sheds in the fields between Eye and Pecks Farm.

There were several crashes near the airfield. The top picture shows a USAF P51 Mustang crashed into what was then a village a shop and is now a private house on the corner of Rectory Rd and the Eye road.

Below - Church farm barns, Brome, with American officers shortly after their arrival in 1942. All were trained in airfield and building construction. Their living quarters were cottages in Potash Lane, Eye. These were demolished afterwards.

In 1939, well before the arrival of US forces, the RAF was busy in the area. This picture shows the aftermath of a crash of a Bristol Blenheim medium bomber which crashed in 1940 halfway along Buck Lane, near a guidance beacon.

Corporal Eddie Guilian was one of many British servicemen to be stationed in the area before the arrival of US forces. Being far from home they were made welcome with evenings at the village hall where refreshments were served by the local ladies. Eddie met and married Joan West of Ivy House before he landed in France on D-day + 2 and took his Bren Gun carrier though to Germany in 1945. His carrier sustained a direct hit but he was luckily unscathed.

This picture was taken in 1945 and shows a Flying Fortress crew on Eye airfield with, standing far right, a young Peter West in full parachute gear. The author flew several times with USAF crews in B-17 Flying Fortresses.

After WW2 ended East Anglia remained on the front line during the Cold War. In July 1960 an RAF Victor bomber from Honington, part of the UK's nuclear deterrent flight, crashed onto Oakley Plains after running into trouble over Diss. Three of the five crew were killed, although four had managed to eject. The picture is believed to show the plane's captain, Fl Lt Mudford, in the immediate aftermath.

Brome village well was the only source of drinking water until the 1950s. Roof water was used for washing. The well is today capped and sits near the village sign in front of the Almshouses. The house opposite, on the left, was at one time The Buck public house.

The last working horse on Church Farm was a Suffolk punch bred in 1960. It is pictured here in front of the tiled-roofed building which was the stable block of the original Brome rectory – before The Oaksmere was built – demolished in the early 1800s. The large building in the background is the old tithe barn.

J. WORBEY, R PRIOR, J. Healey, A. Peart
Builder   Chairman   Builder   Builder

The American memorial in front of the Village Hall was built as a replica of the old village well. It was opened in 1985 and was the scene of several memorial events and reunions until recently. From left to right: J. Worbey, builder. R. Prior, chairman. J. Healey, builder. A. Peart, builder.

One of the last photos to be taken of the old Brome Hall, becoming a ruin. After its occupation by the military in 1939-44 it remained vacant and fell into disrepair. The estate, much reduced from its prime, was bought by Oliver West in 1953 and, with no financial support for its preservation, the house was demolished in 1962 and replaced by the modern Brome Hall.

For centuries Brome and Oakley were separate, independent villages with their own administration and parish churches. The two villages were merged under one administrative Parish Council in 1982. The decline in postwar churchgoing also meant it was difficult to sustain St Mary's Brome and St Nicholas' Oakley as two separate, independent churches and they, together with All Saints Stuston and St Margaret's Thrandeston, were merged into one benefice in 1973. Since then the Benefice has expanded to include Burgate, Wortham and Palgrave. More recently the discussion has considered even further local consolidation. This picture shows the service to mark the initial grouping with two churchwardens present from each of the four churches including, third from right, the author, Peter West.

Chapter 5 – The Friendly invasion

When war was declared in 1939 the centuries old patterns of life were about to be massively disrupted. Within a week of the September 3rd declaration of war a unit of the Middlesex Territorial Regiment arrived and set up their HQ at Warren Hills farm. There were five detachments in the area with searchlights, machine guns and rifles but no anti-aircraft artillery. One unit was near Buck Lane. They were initially housed in tents but by winter wooden huts had been built for their accommodation.

At the same time the RAF arrived in the village with a very powerful beacon, visible from the coast. Its role was to guide aircraft returning from Germany to their home base. It was moved around different locations to confuse German aircraft. But in the autumn of 1940, with the leaves coming off the trees, the beacon accidentally shone on the Warren Hills camp and a cruising German plane promptly dropped five bombs. Fortunately the bombs missed the camp but landed in the chicken runs. There were no human casualties but several hens made the ultimate sacrifice for their country.

Not all airborne danger was posed by the Luftwaffe. In 1940 an RAF Blenheim light bomber was trying to make its way back to Wattisham when it got lost after coming off the North Sea. After running out of fuel it crash landed at night. There were no casualties but the crash woke the occupants of Warren Hill, who welcomed the fliers back to English soil with a cup of tea.

Eye airfield

Later in the war we got our own airfield. Construction of Eye airfield, part of which is in Brome after which it was initially named, started in 1942. It was built by US Engineer Battalions. All 800 of the construction GIs were black, which caused a stir in the local pubs! They had arrived in Southampton by ship and travelled to Diss by train.

My father, who was a special constable in Eye at the time, had already been informed that the troops were from the southern states in America and that they were all black. The officers, who were white, were the technicians and were to be housed in commandeered farm cottages in Eye, later demolished to make way for the runway.

At this time segregation was the norm in the southern US states. The local police, including my father, who had already established there would be no segregation on his farm, had informed the US officers there was no such thing as segregation in England. Jamaicans and English airmen were already working side by side at Pulham. This was readily agreed. The discussion took place in August. According to the papers recently released this issue was not resolved until the end of September by Washington and London. Brome led the way again!

The engineers got a warm welcome from a German aircraft straight after their arrival. Their Army-issue sleeping bags needed padding for comfort and the farm provided them with loads of straw from the recent threshing. But the soldiers had not been told of the blackout rules and not being used to the cold at night they set fire to the straw for warmth. A German aircraft flying overhead at the time dropped a canister of incendiary bombs, which exploded over the area. Luckily there were no casualties but a bit of panic. Their training in the States had been in construction, not warfare.

The Americans had to wait for their equipment to arrive and in their spare time they soon integrated with the local community. Most of them were from farming communities in the southern US states and were rural workers. Apart from segregation, living conditions were similar.

When I was working in the fields I would drive the horses and farm wagons and would go to their camp area to get the hay for the horses. The Americans would always load the cart for me. One told me he had never seen a white boy working in the fields at home.

With the Americans in our midst the whole area was a hive of activity. Fields in Brome, Eye and Yaxley became an airfield with three runways, hangars and, eventually, accommodation for 2,500 airmen. The base had running water and a sewerage system – something the villages lacked for several years to come.

The 490 BG

The airfield was handed over to the USAF 490 Bomb Group in 1944. The 490 flew close support for the June D-day landings in their B-24 Liberators. Shortly after these were replaced by B-17 Flying Fortresses for longer range missions.

Brome and Oakley villagers, including the children, mixed freely with the servicemen. Some children ran errands for the men and some tell poignant stories of returning to the barracks to complete the errand only to find that hut space cleared out and empty.

Probably the worse thing was to hear damaged plans limping back to base after having been hit in action over France or Germany. We can only imagine the thoughts of those young men who had nursed their plane back to Brome getting ready to crash land.

These were not uncommon incidents and in two years of active service there were a number of fatal crashes. In 1944 the cattle yard at Pecks Farm was destroyed by bombs jettisoned by two Flying Fortresses which collided. Seventeen of the twenty crew were killed with three survivors parachuting to safety. A Liberator crashed in a pall of black smoke near the Brome Swan public house while across the triangle a Mustang crashed into the village shop on the Brome-Eye crossroads.

I witness a crash

On a summer's day - 29th July 1944 – I witnessed a four-engined Liberator approaching Eye airfield with only two engines working and another failing. It failed to make it and glided through a row of oak tree-tops before crashing onto the A140 outside Brome Swan. I biked towards it quickly and although the plane was ablaze all the crew has managed to escape the inferno. Sadly two died shortly after they were taken to Brome airfield hospital near the Oaksmere.

It is difficult to explain just how much activity was taking place at this time. The RAF flew overhead most nights and on Eye airfield aircraft engines would warm up well before dawn ready for daylight raids.

The US 8th Airforce, all based in East Anglia at the time, kept detailed records. On that day alone 1,228 B-17 and B-24 bombers flew to eight targets and dropped 2,957 tons of bombs. Seventeen aircraft did not return and nine crew members were killed, including the two in Brome. A further 26 crew were injured and 153 were missing in action. The bombers were escorted by 755 fighters, of which seven went missing with their pilots.

All told there were eight aircraft crashes in Brome resulting in the loss of 26 American airmen and four British workmen. Two of the aircraft were RAF; in 1940 a Blenheim ran out of fuel and a Whitley bomber landed with bombs aboard which closed Buck Lane for a week. Both planes landed near the Beacon as they were able to see the ground in the dark.

A Flying Fortress from Thorpe Abbotts crashed on Brome Road killing its 13-member crew and 4 workmen. The other crashes were during take-off or landing.

There were also more routine disruptions to deal with. The decision was taken to build several plane parking bays on the Thrandeston side of the A140, a major road even then. Although there were many fewer vehicles than today this layout necessitated stopping all the traffic on the A140 every time a plane was moved to and from parking. Those original parking bays are still visible today.

The 490 returned to the USA in July 1945. Whatever those young men thought they were fighting for, their time in Brome and Eye seems to have left a good impression. In 1985, forty years after the end of the war, a memorial shelter was opened in front of the village hall to remember the presence of and sacrifices by the 490. In 1995 a 50th anniversary celebration was held in the village attended by several original 490 servicemen who had served here in 1944-45. Many were accompanied by their families and they all remembered their time here fondly. A memorial plaque was unveiled in Brome Church in honour of the casualties of the 490 BG.

The not so friendly visitors

Due west of Brome is Redgrave Park. Redgrave Hall was built around the same time as Brome Hall by Sir Nicholas Bacon. A prisoner of war camp was built in the grounds in WW2 which initially housed Italian prisoners then Germans. The last group to arrive were Ukrainians who had joined German forces against Russia. Some of these claimed political asylum but many were returned to Russia.

Redgrave Hall was also a military hospital for the US forces in 1943-45. It was staffed by the 65th General Hospital, US army division, mainly American women volunteers. It featured 1450 beds. Redgrave Hall was demolished in 1946.

Twelve nurses from that Redgrave hospital attended the 1997 opening by Queen Elizabeth II of the American Air Museum at Duxford. They also visited Eye airfield and Brome memorial before dining at the Oaksmere. The photo shows Frank Hollidge, Lay Reader, at the dinner.

While much of the groundwork of the airfield remains to this day the site has become an industrial estate providing jobs other than farming. But the agricultural connections remain; in addition to several food processing plants the site also hosts a power plant designed to produce electricity from burning chicken litter.

Meanwhile village life continues. Few of its residents work on local farms, although until recently a farm worker could look forward to a Medal for 50 years' service – usually presented at the Norfolk or Suffolk agricultural shows. There will be few, if any, of those awarded now.

Some residents work from home, some locally and some commute further afield, even London. But having lost its pub the social heart of the village remains the village hall. Here the community life of the village carries on, with old and new friends getting together for a good catch-up with a glass of something or a meal, commemorate important events or to manage the affairs of the village. Long may it continue.